W9-AXB-006

Gel

Sarah Michelle Gellar

by
Cynthia Laslo

HIGH
interest
books

Children's Press
A Division of Grolier Publishing
New York / London / Hong Kong / Sydney
Danbury, Connecticut

Photo Credits: Cover, pp. 4, 6, 9, 10, 18, 20, 25, 28, 30, 31, 32 © Everett collection; pp. 12, 16 © Burstein/Globe Photos Inc.; p. 15 © Ed Gellar/Globe Photos Inc.; pp. 26, 36 © Lisa Rose/Globe Photos Inc.; p. 35 © Fitzroy Barr/Globe Photos Inc.

Visit Children's Press on the Internet at:
http://publishing.grolier.com

Library of Congress Cataloging-in-Publication Data

Laslo, Cynthia, 1943–
    Sarah Michelle Gellar / by Cynthia Laslo.
        p. cm. — (Celebrity bios)
    Includes bibliographical references and index.
    Summary: Traces the life and career of the woman who stars in the television program "Buffy the Vampire Slayer."
        ISBN 0-516-23326-2 (lib. bdg.) — ISBN 0-516-23526-5 (pbk.)
        1. Gellar, Sarah Michelle, 1977– . Juvenile literature.
    2. Actors—United States Biography Juvenile literature.
    [1. Gellar, Sarah Michelle, 1977– . 2. Actors and actresses. 3. Women Biography.]   I. Title. II. Series.
    PN2287.G46L37 2000   99-41086
                                                 CIP

CONTENTS

CHAPTER ONE

Sarah's Success

"It's amazing, it's incredible, and the best part for me is that I'm doing what I've always wanted to do." —Sarah Michelle Gellar in an interview with "Access Hollywood"

The night is dark, but a full moon shines down on the peaceful Sunnydale cemetery. Suddenly the silence is broken by a loud crash, as the door to an old crypt opens and falls to the ground. A vampire slinks out, hungry for his first victim of the evening. Without warning, he is kicked from behind and thrown to the ground. Before the vampire can fight back, a beautiful young woman spins and flips

Sarah Michelle Gellar as Buffy

through the air, landing on his chest. She plunges a wooden stake into the evil creature's heart. The dying vampire slowly crumbles into a pile of dust. The young woman strides away to continue her graveyard patrol.

Sarah's Success

The young woman is Buffy Summers, of the hit television series "Buffy the Vampire Slayer." The actress who plays Buffy is the multitalented Sarah Michelle Gellar (ge-LAR). The show is funny, smart, and even a bit scary, and Sarah is the star at the center of it all.

Each week, millions of people tune in to the WB network to watch Buffy defend the town of Sunnydale against vampires, demons, and other forms of evil. Battling creatures twice her size comes easily to Buffy. All this fighting requires a lot of practice for Sarah, though!

How did this young woman from New York City come to be known as the "Vampire Slayer"? Sarah worked very hard to achieve her success. She appeared in TV commercials at an early age, and moved on to small television roles. Gradually, Sarah worked her way up to larger parts. She gained experience in movies, soap operas, and on the Broadway stage.

YOUNG PERFORMER

Sarah Michelle Gellar was born in New York City on April 14, 1977. Her parents divorced in 1984. Her mother, Rosellen Gellar, who was a kindergarten teacher, raised her alone. Sarah, an only child, always knew that she wanted to be an actress.

One day, a talent agent spotted four-year-old Sarah eating in a local restaurant. Sarah was immediately hired to act in a Burger King commercial. That was the first of more than 100 commercials in which she has appeared.

When she was six years old, Sarah appeared in "An Invasion of Privacy," a television movie about community justice. One year later, she hit the big screen in the movie *Over the Brooklyn Bridge*. She played the daughter of a coffee shop owner who dreams of running a fancy New York City restaurant.

In 1986, Sarah's career began to take off. Sarah was chosen to play Emily, the daughter of Robert Urich's character, on the popular television series

"Spenser: For Hire." She then decided to try out for the Broadway stage. At age ten, she was cast opposite Matthew Broderick and Eric Stolz in *The Widow Claire*, a play about the relationship between a young widow and a college student. Over the next year-and-a-half, Sarah also acted in small roles in feature films, including *High Stakes* and *Funny Farm*, which starred Chevy Chase.

Sarah was only six years old when she starred in the TV movie "An Invasion of Privacy."

In 1989, twelve-year-old Sarah got the chance to cohost a new television talk show called "Girl Talk." The program gave Sarah a lot of exposure,

From left to right: Sarah Michelle Gellar, Tom Carroll,
and Kristy Barbera in "Swan's Crossing"

and the next year she got a part in the TV movie
"A Woman Named Jackie." In the award-winning
movie, Sarah played the teenage Jacqueline
Bouvier Kennedy, the wife of President John F.

Kennedy. That same year, fourteen-year-old Sarah won a starring role on a new teen soap opera called "Swans Crossing." Sarah played the lead character, Sydney Rutledge. Although the show was canceled after only one season, Sarah already had a fan club! People were definitely taking notice of this talented young actress.

SCHOOL DAYS

As Sarah worked steadily in movies and television, she attended school as any other young person. Although Sarah was successful in her professional life, she felt like an outcast in her private junior high school in New York. She didn't feel as though she had anything in common with her wealthy classmates. When *Soap Opera Digest* asked Sarah about her life in junior high, she explained, "Many students were used to having everything handed to them on a silver platter. Everything I got I worked hard for and got on my own."

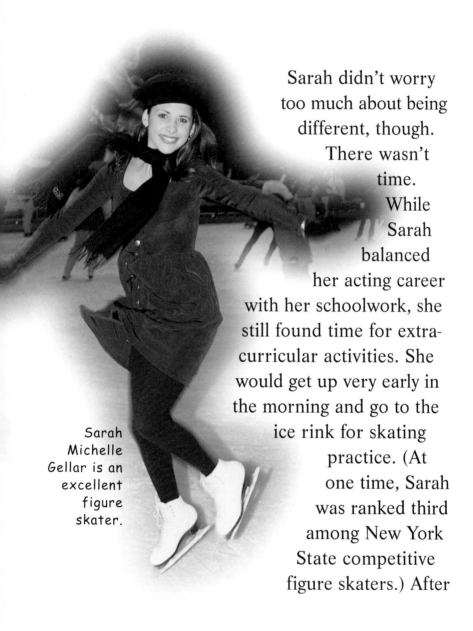

Sarah
Michelle
Gellar is an
excellent
figure
skater.

Sarah didn't worry too much about being different, though. There wasn't time. While Sarah balanced her acting career with her schoolwork, she still found time for extra-curricular activities. She would get up very early in the morning and go to the ice rink for skating practice. (At one time, Sarah was ranked third among New York State competitive figure skaters.) After practice, Sarah would head off to school. After school, she would go on auditions, where she would try out for different film, television, or theater roles. Sarah often followed her auditions with sessions of tae kwon do, a Korean martial art that involves kicking and punching moves. Little did Sarah know then how this skill would help her in her future role as Buffy!

Did you know?

One of Sarah's favorite books is Dr. Seuss's *There's a Wocket in My Pocket* because of this line: "like the GELLAR in the CELLAR."

When Sarah finally moved from junior high to high school, she was able to fit in more comfortably with the other students. She attended two special New York City high schools—the Professional

Children's School and LaGuardia High School for the Performing Arts. Both schools were designed for young performers like Sarah, helping them attend school when their work schedules made going to class difficult. Sarah's classmates were also young artists: actors, dancers, singers, musicians, and other performers. Sarah no longer felt awkward or different. She was around people who were like her.

Sarah even met a future co-star at the Professional Children's School. Ryan Phillippe was one of Sarah's classmates. Later in life, Ryan and Sarah would star together in two movies, *I Know What You Did Last Summer* and *Cruel Intentions.*

A TALENTED GIRL

Sarah was just a fifteen-year-old high school student when she got her big break. In February 1993, Sarah joined the cast of the successful soap opera "All My Children." Her character was Kendall Hart, the daughter of the famous TV

Sarah Michelle and Susan Lucci

character, Erica Kane (played by actress Susan Lucci). Kendall was a wicked daughter who spent most of her time trying to wreck her mother's life. It was a very challenging role for Sarah. Working with the well-known actress Susan Lucci made Sarah nervous. Though Sarah had been acting for several years, this role really was the chance of a lifetime.

Sarah won a Daytime Emmy in 1995 for Outstanding Younger Performer for her role on "All My Children."

Sarah may have been nervous, but viewers liked her work right away. In 1994, only one year after Sarah started on "All My Children," she was nominated for a Daytime Emmy Award for Outstanding Younger Performer. She didn't win the award that year. The following year, on the same night as her senior prom, Sarah did win the Emmy! What did she do? "I actually had to decide," Sarah explained in an interview with *Mademoiselle*. "Do I go to the prom or do I go to the Emmys? So I went to the Emmys and to the prom after-party."

The day after accepting the award, seventeen-year-old Sarah made one of the most important decisions of her life. She announced that she was leaving "All My Children" to pursue a career in Hollywood. In 1995, Sarah and her mom moved to Los Angeles. Sarah wasn't sure if she would make it in Hollywood. For almost a year, she went on audition after audition and wasn't offered any parts. Then along came a role that would change Sarah's career forever.

CHAPTER TWO

Hard Work

"I've been working Monday through Thursday on 'Buffy' and Friday, Saturday, and Sunday on Scream 2. But hey, this is the time in my life when I'm supposed to work like a dog. I'll relax when I'm old!"
—Sarah in an interview with react

In 1996, Sarah auditioned for a new television series based on the 1992 movie *Buffy The Vampire Slayer*. The movie, which starred Luke Perry from "Beverly Hills, 90210," had been a huge hit with young audiences. Joss Whedon, the man who created the movie, was also creating the

Sarah uses her knowledge of martial arts in her role as Buffy.

Sarah performs most of Buffy's athletic
moves herself.

TV series. At first, Sarah was cast as Cordelia,
Buffy's stuck-up friend at school. Sarah knew in
her heart, though, that she would make the perfect

vampire slayer. She continued to audition and finally captured the lead role of Buffy Summers.

The character Buffy fights vampires and demons using her wits and her kickboxing skills. She runs, punches, and spins with incredible speed and control. In playing Buffy, Sarah draws on her abilities both as an actress and an athlete. Buffy's more dangerous stunts are performed by a stuntwoman, but Sarah performs most of the character's moves herself. All these stunts can be very tiring, especially when Sarah works anywhere from twelve to seventeen hours a day, several days a week. Often she has to work through the night to tape graveyard scenes. It would be a challenge for any actress. Fortunately, Sarah was prepared for the challenge.

STAYING FIT

How does Sarah stay in shape for all those stunts? Her workout routine is not easy, but she has been an athlete for many years. Long before

Sarah got the role of Buffy, she had a very active lifestyle. In addition to figure skating, Sarah earned a brown belt in tae kwon do, which she has studied for more than eleven years.

Sarah's current routine includes working out at the gym three or four times a week. Sometimes she's too busy to get to the gym that often, so she works out at home using a minitrampoline, tread-mill, and free weights. Sarah also enjoys roller-blading, water skiing, and yoga, but she must also practice gymnastics and kickboxing for her work as Buffy.

In addition to all that exercise, Sarah is also extremely careful about what she eats. She doesn't eat sugar or dairy products, and she avoids French fries and other greasy foods. Sarah has found that eating small meals several times a day helps her to stay energetic. She loves eating healthy foods, such as veggie burgers and pasta. Sarah knows that with such a busy schedule, it's important for her to eat right and take vitamins every day.

NEW OPPORTUNITIES

By its second season on the air, "Buffy The Vampire Slayer" was the most-watched show on the WB network. "Buffy" led the way for the creation of other shows for young audiences, such as "Dawson's Creek" and "Felicity."

The success of "Buffy The Vampire Slayer" also created a lot of interest in Sarah Michelle Gellar. Sarah has been able to continue with her tinue with her career in movies. In 1996, she tried out for a part in the horror movie *I Know What You Did Last Summer*. It starred some of today's hottest young

Did you know?

Sarah's life has always been busy—she's carried a pager since she was in the seventh grade!

actors, including Jennifer Love Hewitt, Freddie Prinze, Jr., and Ryan Phillippe. Kevin Williamson, who was responsible for the hit movie *Scream* and the TV series "Dawson's Creek," wrote the script. Sarah won the role of Helen Shivers,

Did you know?

Sarah loves to sing karaoke.

the girl who is crowned the Queen of the Croaker Festival in a small town in Maine.

At first, Sarah found it difficult to play the part of Helen because unlike Buffy, Helen wasn't able to defend herself against the killer. Sarah explained to *Mr. Showbiz*, "It was a little hard at first, just because of my training, and what I'm used to on a day-to-day basis [with 'Buffy']. But that's part of acting." Sarah's acting was so good in fact, that she won two

I Know What You Did Last Summer starred, from left to right: Jennifer Love Hewitt, Ryan Phillippe, Sarah Michelle Gellar, and Freddie Prinze, Jr.

If you're going
to bury the truth,
make sure
it stays buried.

I KNOW
WHAT YOU DID
LAST SUMMER

In 1998, Sarah won a Blockbuster movie award for her performance in *I Know What You Did Last Summer*.

awards for her work in *I Know What You Did Last Summer*. She received the MTV award for Best Breakthrough Performance and a

Hard Work

Blockbuster Movie Award for Best Supporting Actress in a Horror Movie.

Sarah's next picture that year was the scary thriller *Scream 2*. Most young actresses wanted to snag a part in the follow-up to the hit horror flick, *Scream*. Sarah was one of the lucky few who was chosen, along with former *Scream* stars Neve Campbell from "Party of Five" and Courteney Cox from "Friends." Sarah played Cici Cooper, a sorority sister at the college where the movie is set. The part was small, and her character didn't live for very long, but Sarah enjoyed being in the film. "[*Scream 2*] is action, it's drama, it's horror, it's comedy, it's all those things," Sarah told *Dungeon of Darkness*, "and when you are my age, it is the best opportunity."

Acting in these films was exciting for Sarah, but it also meant that her schedule was very diffi-cult. The day after she finished filming *I Know What You Did Last Summer* in North Carolina, Sarah flew to Atlanta, Georgia, to begin filming

Scream 2. The second season of "Buffy" began shooting at the same time. Sarah had to fly back and forth between Atlanta and Los Angeles until she had finished filming her part in *Scream 2.*

I Know What You Did Last Summer and *Scream 2* were two of the biggest hits of 1997. The success of these films and of the "Buffy" series meant that Sarah would be able to audition for bigger and better roles in other movies.

IN THE LEAD

The following year, during a break in taping "Buffy," Sarah acted in two more movies. This time, however, Sarah was playing the lead roles. The first movie was *Simply Irresistible.* Sarah starred as Amanda Shelton, a restaurant chef, who tries to win the heart of a businessman played by Sean Patrick Flanery.

Her second movie released in 1999 was *Cruel Intentions.* Sarah played the lead character, Kathryn Merteuil, and Ryan Phillippe played her

Sarah Michelle Gellar had a supporting role in one of the hottest movies of 1997, *Scream 2.*

Sarah Michelle Gellar played the lead role in the romantic comedy *Simply Irresistible*.

half-brother, Sebastian Valmont. The role was a big change for Sarah. Instead of playing a likable teenager, such as Buffy, Sarah was playing a cruel and heartless young woman. When "Entertainment Tonight" asked Sarah if it was fun to play the part of Kathryn, she replied, "It was something different; it was a challenge. It was a character that I haven't really tackled yet. And very different from what I do [on 'Buffy']."

Sarah Michelle Gellar starred with former high school classmate Ryan Phillippe in 1999's *Cruel Intentions*.

CHAPTER THREE

Fans and the Future

"Buffy is not the prettiest girl in school; she's not the most popular, and she's not the smartest. She makes mistakes; she makes good decisions and bad decisions. [Buffy is a character] people can look up to." —Sarah in an interview with *Dungeon of Darkness*

"Buffy the Vampire Slayer" has fans all over the world. Many of these fans are also fans of Sarah Michelle Gellar. Sarah enjoys the success of her career, but admits that everything has happened very quickly. "You don't really have time to stop

and think about it," she told "Access Hollywood."
"Your life changes . . . and it's very hard to adapt
to that change."

Sarah has gotten used to people asking for her
autograph everywhere she goes, but sometimes it
prevents her from doing the things she likes to
do. When Sarah travels, her suitcases have a fake
name on them so that no one will try to steal
them. Once she was spotted at a restaurant, and
so many people surrounded her that she had to
escape through the loading dock!

ONLINE AUDIENCE

Sarah's fans are incredibly devoted, and many of
them share their enthusiasm on the Internet.
More than 300 Web sites have been created by
Sarah's fans. The Web sites provide a lot of information about Sarah. They include pictures and
sometimes chat rooms and message boards where
fans can talk to one another. What do Sarah's fans
discuss online? They chat about the characters on

Sarah has a great sense of style.

Sarah at a Hollywood movie premiere

"Buffy." They talk about what they think will happen next on the show. They also talk about Sarah's clothes and lifestyle.

SARAH'S STYLE

Sarah has a terrific style of her own. She is often photographed at movie openings and parties. She is a fan of very stylish designers. She likes wearing funky outfits by Vivienne Tam and Betsey Johnson. Her favorites are vintage clothing, long leather coats, tank tops, and skirts. When she played Kathryn in *Cruel Intentions,* many people noticed her costumes, which were very short and tight. Sarah told "Entertainment Tonight" that even the shoes were tight:

Did you know?

Sarah's least favorite foods are meatloaf and liver.

"The minute they called 'Cut!' I was like, 'Someone get me sneakers, please!'"

Sarah has definitely gone through some wild periods in her life. She once wore a ring in her belly button. She has five earring holes in each earlobe. "I went through this crazy phase when I was younger," Sarah told *People*. "I would dye my hair a different color every week. I wanted to be a really goth [gothic] teenager." Sarah also has a tattoo on her ankle. It's the Tao symbol for patience. "It's about life patience," she

Did you know?

In 1999, *TV Guide Online* readers named Sarah Sexiest Female, Best-Dressed Female, Best Teen Character, Favorite Female Hairdo, as well as choosing "Buffy the Vampire Slayer" as the Best Sci-Fi Fantasy Show.

explained to *InStyle*. "If you follow the path you truly believe in, you'll be rewarded."

THE FUTURE

Sarah's patience and hard work have certainly been rewarded. Sarah recently bought her own house in Los Angeles, California, which she shares with her dog, a Maltese named Thor. Her work on television continues as "Buffy the Vampire Slayer" enters another season. She's a model for Maybelline costmetics. She's also hard at work putting together a children's mythology book.

Though she's only twenty-three years old, Sarah has many movie roles and awards to her credit. It takes a lot of work for an actress to make it to the top and stay there. Sarah has fought very hard to get where she is today. Sarah's a rising star, and it looks as though she's going to be a Hollywood actress for a long time!

TIMELINE

1977	• Sarah Michelle Gellar is born on April 14 in New York City.
1982	• Sarah is hired for her first commercial (Burger King).
1983	• Sarah's first TV movie "An Invasion of Privacy" airs.
1984	• Sarah's first big-screen movie *Over the Brooklyn Bridge* is released.
1986	• Sarah appears on TV's "Spenser: For Hire."
1987	• Sarah debuts on Broadway in *The Widow Claire.*
1988	• Sarah appears in the movie *Funny Farm.*
1989	• Sarah appears in the movie *High Stakes* and co-hosts "Girl Talk" on TV.
1990–1991	• Sarah plays Sydney Rutledge on the soap opera "Swans Crossing." • Sarah plays Jacqueline Bouvier in the TV movie "A Woman Named Jackie."
1993	• Sarah cast as Kendall Hart on the soap opera "All My Children."
1994	• Sarah is nominated for a Daytime Emmy Award for Outstanding Younger Performer.

1995	• Sarah wins the Daytime Emmy Award on the same night as her high school prom.
	• Sarah announces she is leaving "All My Children" to pursue a movie career.
1996	• Sarah is cast as Buffy on TV's "Buffy the Vampire Slayer."
1997	• Sarah played a spoiled teenager in the TV movie *Beverly Hills Family Robinson*.
	• Sarah plays Helen Shivers in *I Know What You Did Last Summer*.
	• Sarah plays Cici Cooper in *Scream 2*.
1998	• Sarah wins a Blockbuster Movie Award for Best Supporting Actress in a Horror Movie for *I Know What You Did Last Summer*.
	• Sarah is the voice of a Gwendy doll in the movie *Small Soldiers*.
	• Sarah is the voice of Marie in an episode of Fox's "King of the Hill."
1999	• Sarah plays Amanda Shelton in *Simply Irresistible*.
	• Sarah plays Kathryn Merteuil in *Cruel Intentions*.
	• Sarah hosts TV's "Saturday Night Live."

FACT SHEET

Name	Sarah Michelle Gellar
Born	April 14, 1977
Birthplace	New York City
Family	Parents divorced; Mother: Rosellen; no brothers or sisters
Sign	Aries
Height	5' 3"
Hair	Dark Brown (dyed blonde for "Buffy")
Eyes	Green

Favorites

Actors	Tom Cruise, John Cusack
Actress	Stockard Channing
Book	*Gone With the Wind*
Color	Red
Foods	Pasta, Chinese food, veggie burgers
Movies	*Heathers, Grosse Point Blank*
TV Shows	"Seinfeld," "Party of Five"
Music	Lauryn Hill, Billy Joel, Alanis Morissette
Pet	Thor (Maltese terrier)
Scent	Vanilla
Hobbies	Ice skating, scuba diving, shopping
Sports	Ice skating, football
Team	New York Giants (football)

NEW WORDS

audition a try-out performance to win a role

breakthrough new discovery

Broadway the section of New York City where theaters present professional dramas and musicals

crypt tomb

Emmy award an award given for outstanding achievement in television

kickboxing a modern sport that combines rapid kicking movements with boxing moves

martial arts a form of combat or self-defense, such as karate or judo

nomination selection of someone for an award

outcast someone who doesn't fit in with others

ratings numbers that evaluate the performance and audience size of a particular TV show

role a character or part played by a performer

season a specific period of the year when a television series airs

soap opera a television drama that airs in continuous episodes

sorority a social organization of female college
students

tae kwon do a Korean art of self-defense

Tao from Taoism, a Chinese religion

Web site a computer page on the Internet

FOR FURTHER READING

Baker, Jennifer. *Sarah Michelle Gellar.* New York: Simon & Schuster, 1998.

Genge, Ngaire. *Buffy Chronicles: The Unofficial Guide to Buffy the Vampire Slayer.* New York: Crown Publishing Group, Inc., 1998.

Golden, Christopher and Nancy Holder. *Buffy the Vanpire Slayer: Sunnydale High Yearbook.* New York: Pocket Books, 1999.

Stafford, Nikki. *Bite Me! Sarah Michelle Gellar and Buffy the Vampire Slayer.* Milford, CT: LPC InBook, 1998.

Tracy, Kathleen. *The Girl's Got Bite: The Unofficial Guide to Buffy's World.* Los Angeles: Renaissance Books, 1998.

RESOURCES

Web Sites

Buffy Chat Room
http://chat.warnerbros.com
Discuss Sarah and the latest "Buffy" episodes here.

Buffy the Vampire Slayer
www.buffy.com
The official site for the WB television show.

Sarah's IMDB Page
http://us.imdb.com/Name?Gellar,+Sarah+Michelle
This Internet Movie Database page has complete information on all of Sarah's movies and TV appearances, as well as biographical material.

You can also write to Sarah at the following address:

Sarah Michelle Gellar
c/o "Buffy the Vampire Slayer"
c/o The Warner Brothers Television Network
4000 Warner Blvd.
Burbank, CA 91522

INDEX

ABOUT THE AUTHOR

Cynthia Laslo was born in Norway and moved to Iowa with her parents in 1955. After high school, she taught English as a second language in the school system of Maricao, Puerto Rico.